DISCOVERING
Out of Doors

G/L Regal Venture Books
A Division of G/L Publications
Glendale, California, USA

If you have a yard, a garden
or a park nearby,
you can go exploring.
You can discover
some of the amazing things
God has made.
And you can discover something new
every day!

You will have to get up
early in the morning
to see a beautiful surprise
like this one God has made.
These are drops of dew
caught in a spider's web.
When the sun is out
the dew will dry up and disappear.

Caterpillars sometimes make long threads
and hang on them from the trees.
Sometimes you will see
a caterpillar on the ground.
But mostly they are hiding
among the leaves they eat.

Some caterpillars are hairy.
Some are smooth.
This hairy caterpillar is on a
hairy leaf.
The smooth caterpillar is on a
smooth leaf.

Here is a dandelion.
God made dandelions
to grow little parachutes
for carrying their seeds
to new ground.
Under each little parachute
is one dandelion seed.
One puff – and all the little parachutes

fly away with their seeds.

You may find a spiky brown ball
– like this one –
among the leaves.
It is a hedgehog hiding
or sleeping.
If you set out a saucer of milk
and are very very still
you may see him uncurl
and have a drink.
When he uncurls, you can see
his little pointed nose
and bright eyes.

God made flowers to grow
in all kinds of places.
Sometimes they grow in cracks of walls.
Sometimes they even push their way
up through concrete!
Wherever flowers grow
they make God's world beautiful.

You can recognize a robin by his red breast feathers. He is a friendly bird and likes to live near people.
If you see a bird
with twigs or straw in his beak,
watch him carefully.

You may discover where he is building his nest. God helps him know just the right way to build it.

If you find a big flat stone,
lift it up and look underneath.
You may see some little creatures who
make their home there, like this beetle

and this slippery slug.

Look up at the clouds.
They are made of thousands

and thousands of tiny water drops.
Clouds are different shapes
on different days. Little white clouds
mean God is sending a clear day.
Big dark clouds mean a rainy day.
Long, thin, wispy clouds mean that winds
are blowing high up in the sky.
Sometimes on warm days,
there are no clouds at all.

God made these field mice
a color that is
not easy to see.
They are the same color
as the fields where they live.
Field mice are about the size
of a large nut.

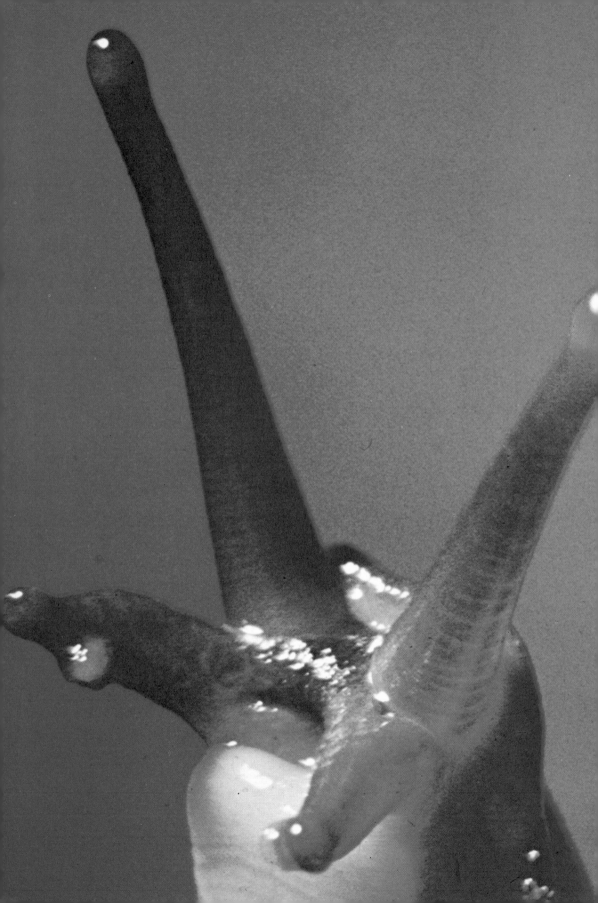

Is this a space monster?
No, it's a garden snail!
God made his horns
to help the snail feel
where he is going.
If you gently put your finger

near his horns,
he will pull them right back to
his head.

Some day you may see a butterfly
hatching from its cocoon. At first,
the butterfly's wings are all folded
and crumpled. A few hours later
his wings will be dry and opened out.
Then you can see the lovely
pattern and colors of his wings.
24

Have you seen any
green prickly things
– like these –
lying under the trees?

When you open one of these
green prickly seeds, you find
a shiny brown chestnut inside.
God planned for these prickly seeds
to grow into chestnut trees
when they are planted in the ground.

God's world is full of surprises.
See what YOU can find
when you are out of doors.
Say thank you to God
for this wonderful world
He has made for us
to explore and enjoy.

"The earth belongs to God! Every-
thing in all the world is his."
Psalm 24:1